I0078763

# Anatomy Of Being A Misfit

## A Study

Aanya Saxena

BookLeaf
Publishing

India | USA | UK

Made with ❤ on the BookLeaf Publishing Platform
www.bookleafpub.in
www.bookleafpub.com

# Dedication

*To the steady oak and the joyful shadow that follows the sun.*

# Preface

This is the ossuary of lost atmospheres. Within, you will not find a narrative, but the radiant residue of a mind adrift between stations. The after-image of a borrowed sigh, the scarred tissue of a conflict that was never mine, the perfect, silent grammar of a dream I was asked to carry. Each entry is a talisman, left not at the altar of a known god, but in the shadowed alcove of a moment that demanded witness.

# Acknowledgements

My gratitude, first, to the silent architects of my world, who built the rooms where these thoughts could safely wander. To the steady pulse of a loyal heart, a companion in the quiet. And to the unforeseen current that provided both the pressure and the channel for these words to find their form.

# 1. Insistent Distance

The sun asked the moon to marry him
The moon tries to hide its addiction.

If the moon said yes, the sun would explode with
happiness
The moon doesn't know that it is the sun's weakness
The moon thinks of all the possibilities
It feels overwhelmed with all the probabilities

If the moon said no, the sun would darken with sadness
It thought about telling him that this was madness
It stops for a second and stares longingly
The entire galaxy pauses and holds its breath patiently

The moon sighs and replies with a 'I don't know'
And so the Milky Way simply continues with its flow
And until today, Saturn keeps the rings
While the moon tries desperately to hide its true
feelings.

So when the sun approaches, the moon hides away
It appears to find a different place to stay
But in reality, the moon just hides and appreciates the
sun's warmth

And eventually that became the universe's norm.

Those rare times when the sun and the moon are in the same sky,
A subtle proposal, the earth must imply.

Every time the sun manages to come close to the moon,
The moon simply turns its back and does not swoon.

Maybe for us.
Or maybe he is selfish,
never wants the sun to lose his shine
as it chases a love so divine.

Every eclipse, a beautiful pair, though temporary.
Perhaps none of this was necessary.

# 2. Axiom of the Scratched Celestial

I was a palimpsest, a vellum skin
Stretched on a green-wood frame, and held within,
The hurried cartography of a child-scribe's hand,
Who charted the coast but not the land?
A map of smiles, a topography of sighs,
With monsters hidden from all eyes.
My skin, thin parchment, showed the ghostly trace
Of every vanished, self-effaced face.

The air was a vitrine of violet glass,
Where every thought was bent to pass
As something sweet, and pale, and pure,
Built on a foundation less than sure.
My voice, a dandelion-clock's brief breath,
Dispersed its seeds to a social death.
I wore a carapace of gossamer thread,
Spun from the living and the dead;
A shining, borrowed, fool's-gold sheen,
To mask the nascent, subterranean queen.

Then came the key of frozen light,
That broke the amethyst of night.
Not with a hammer's brutal blow,

But with a truth that, soft and slow,
Unstitched the seams of my disguise
And showed the truth behind my eyes.
A neutrino, through my leaden shield,
Revealing what I must congeal.

This new light was no gentle dawn;
It was the glare when hope is gone.
The lamp that archaeologists lower
To exhume a lost and latent power.
It showed the forest of my spine,
Petrified, but still divine;
The fossil record of my will,
Resisting some external drill;
The quartz veins where my strength still ran
Beneath the marble of The Plan.

This dawn is not a pastel hue;
It is the white glare, harsh and true,
Of a supernova's final breath,
That writes the scripture of my death.
The death of who I was before,
Upon that strange, interior shore.
The monster on the map, now seen,
Is just a king, a nascent green.

So let the violet vitrine break!
A brighter, colder dawn's awake.
I am not a text for you to gloss,
Nor a potential, tragic loss.
I am the astronomer who reads
The constellation of her needs,
The pulse and rhythm of her star,
This is what we truly are.
The palimpsest, the radiant glow,
The shadow I have learned to know.

# 3. The Cartographer's Lament

I was given a map at birth, etched in silver and gold,
To a city of numbers, a story I was told.
A metropolis of logic, where rivers of reason run straight,
Where every door has a number, and every number, a gate.

But my compass was forged in a different fire,
Its needle points only to my own heart's desire.
It spins for the beauty, the pattern, the art,
But it trembles and faints at the mention of a chart.
The streets on my map are a tangled, wild thread,
And the north that I'm given is somewhere ahead,
Is behind, is below, in a shifting, slow dance,
Leaving logic and sequence no possible chance.

I am a scribe in a library, vast and divine,
But the language they speak is not written in mine.
The glyphs are like spiders that crawl off the page,
In a riot of symbols, a beautiful rage.
Each equation's a sonnet I desperately try to recite,
But the meter is broken, the rhymes don't align,
And the numbers, like rebels, refuse to unite.

They swap their positions, they alter their names,
Leaving chaos and echoes inside of my frame.

I see the great clockwork, the celestial machine,
The planets in orbit, a dance so serene.
I feel its great beauty, its profound, silent grace,
But I cannot count its turns, nor measure its space.
My own inner chronometer ticks to a different, lost star,
Where minutes are mountains and hours are far.
A deadline's a cliff-face, a timeline, a snare,
A labyrinth built from the thinnest of air.

So I build you a city of metaphor and song,
Where the right-angled world can never belong.
I will show you the colors that bloom from the "why?"
And the architecture of clouds that never die.
Do not ask me to measure this love or this pain,
Or to count all the losses, or calculate gain.
My arithmetic is built from the salt of the sea,
And the only true sum is the whole of me.

For the map that they gave me was always a lie,
My kingdom is boundless. My logic is sky.

# 4. The Library of Lost Transitions

They built a library inside my head.
Each shelf was stocked with gold-leaf truth, they said.
The Dewey Decimal system, clean and vast,
A perfect logic meant to always last.
But I am the illiterate librarian here,
Surrounded by a language I revere,
Whose grammar is a cage, whose syntax is a sneer.

Watch me try to read the simplest text:
A map, a clock, the path to what is next.
The letters are like ants that crawl and scatter,
The numbers do not count; they only flatter
The world with an order I cannot possess.
My mind, a frantic, silent S.O.S.,
A constant, quiet, building storm of yes and yes and yes
To the fact of my own failure to correctly guess.

The anger is not lightning, sharp and clear.
It is the low-grade, constant, grinding gear
That turns inside my chest. It is the heat
Of shame for being somehow incomplete.
It is the silent scream into the glass
When someone says, "It's simple. Let it pass.

Just think." I am a swamp of drying gas,
And that small match just makes the silence vast.

I am the saboteur and the betrayed.
I am the foundation that has strayed
From its own blueprint. I am the clumsy ghost
That haunts my own machine, the very most
Responsible for every seized command.
This is a civil war inside the land
Of my own skin. I do not understand
The enemy, because the enemy is my own hand.

And in the social calculus, I fail.
The easy currency, the common grail
Of "meet me on the left," or "ten past three,"
Are ciphers that only serve to underline the plea
My soul is always making: Let me be
Normal for just one day, just one, and see
How it would feel to simply be
Released from this taut, internal tyranny.

So I have built a second, secret shelf,
Behind the brittle facade of my public self.
It holds the real texts, written in the Braille
Of storm clouds, and the slow, forgiving trail
Of snails. It calculates in shades of blue,
And knows the distance by the weight of dew.

It is a kingdom that feels almost true,
And in its wildness, I am almost, quietly, through
With hating the first library I was born into.

# 5. The Anchor

My father's faith was a fortress, firm and fully formed,
A shelter from the sudden storm.
His wisdom was not whispered, but woven in his way,
The guiding glow that guarded me by night and gathered
me by day.

His voice, a calm and constant current, carrying me
along,
As strong as ancient stone, and just as solid in its song.
His presence was a promise, a pillar painted in the
plight,
As deep and dependable as darkness deepening to night.

He stood like a legendary lighthouse on a lonely, rugged
coast,
A sentinel of silent strength, a spectre I could trust the
most.
His hands, a sure and steady charm, to soothe every
alarm,
That built a world from wilderness and guarded me from
harm.

So let this tribute travel on the tongues of time and tide,
For the man who was my map, my moral magnitude, and

my guide.
A life lived with a legacy of love he labored to impart,
A father forged in fire, with a father's flawless heart.

# 6. His Unblinking Creed

He does not arrive on a steed, white and fair,
But in the aftermath of the smoke, standing there.
He is not a knight, with a vow to the sky,
But the shadow that teaches the sunlight to lie.
His armor is not polished; it's battered and scarred,
And his worship is quieter, deeper, and hard.

He did not slay the dragon you thought you must fight,
He simply convinced it to flee in the night.
He didn't proclaim you a queen on a throne,
He just made certain the throne was your own.
His protection is not a loud, clanging boast,
But the silencing of what would trouble you most.

He does not seek to own you, to cage or confine,
For your freedom itself is his holiest shrine.
Your joy is the scripture he's sworn to defend,
Your smile, the only battle he cannot pretend
is beneath his attention. He asks for no land,
Just to be the sharp rock where your weary feet stand.

He is ruin and shelter, a paradox, true,
A storm that has chosen to be gentle for you.
He kneels not in service, but in recognition,

A dark, fallen star acknowledging your mission
to simply exist. And in your mere grace,
He has finally found his one sacred place.

# 7. Echo and the Mapmaker

The wind has booked you a seat on its breath,
to scatter your dust in its galactic wake.
Do not mistake departure for a death;
You are the tremor in the bedrock, the permanent quake.

I have not forgotten the syntax of our noise,
The quiet violence we never gave a voice.
You are not the echo of a passing voice,
But the silence that has stolen my every choice.

If the world should ever ask for your name,
my tongue will have unlearned its ancient claim.
Every scar you sketched, a fossil without fame,
a neutral landmark that I cannot blame.

You were never a guest within my skin;
You are the host, the fever, and the chill.
If every ocean empties, and our tides grow thin,
your current remains the compass of my will.

For this is not a bond that time unties,
it is the ghost note that the stars adore.
And if you ever call to stake your claim,
you'll find I am the silence at the core.

# 8. Celestial Majesty

It is a whirlpool spun from starlight,
A billion brilliant pinpricks, bright.
Against the velvet cloak of night,
A blazing, boundless, royal sight.

A necklace of a trillion suns,
The cosmic dance has just begun.
With sapphire hues and ruby flares,
It hangs in space, beyond all cares.

Nebulae in pastel bloom,
A galactic garden's room,
Where diamond dust and emerald gas,
Illuminate the looking-glass.

It spirals in a grand design,
A miracle of power divine,
A bedazzled, eternal art,
That stirs the soul and stills the heart.

So look upon its jeweled sprawl,
This masterpiece that dwarfs us all,
The most magnificent of schemes,
A kingdom built of light and dreams.

# 9. Secondhand Starlight

I watch them on the silver screen, a soft and gentle fire,
Two borrowed hearts that navigate a map of sweet
desire.
I feel the phantom pull of it, a tide beneath my skin,
A quiet, deep appreciation for the state they're in.

It is not envy, not a want, not a personal, sharp need,
But more a recognition of a beautiful, slow seed.
A knowledge that such grammar exists for souls to
speak,
A language I can comprehend, though I have yet to
speak.

I see the way his glance will fall, the way her laugh lines
grow,
And something in my spirit learns the cadence, soft and
slow.
It feels like reading poetry in a tongue I've never learned,
But understanding every verse as something deeply
earned.

It is a serene and distant joy, a starlight from afar,
A preview of a country where my own feet already are.
For in this borrowed radiance, this cinematic art,

My heart practices the rhythm of a part it knows by heart.

And though my own hands are still empty, and my own screen is bare,
I feel a future chapter rustling in the quiet air.
It doesn't shout. It doesn't ache. It simply lets me know
That somewhere, a love story is waiting for its show.

# 10. Ouroboros

The thought begins again inside the quiet.
Quiet is a cage that feeds the loud.
Loud is the echo of a silent riot.
Riot in the heart becomes a shroud.
Shroud wraps the sense of being void.
Void is the space where hope's destroyed.
Destroyed, I grasp at fractured time.
Time is a ladder I cannot climb.
Climb I must, though limbs feel weak.
Weak is the promise that I seek.
Seek an answer in the grey.
Grey is the color of my day.
Day melts into familiar night.
Night brings no rest, just endless fright.
Fight I do, but with my shadow.
Shadow is the only friend I know.
Know that this loop has no ending.
Ending is just the thought pending.
Pending the start, the new beginning.
Beginning with the same old sinning.
Sinning by staying stuck in dread.
Dread is the poison I am fed.
Fed by the voice that whispers "why".
Why do I help this cycle fly?

Fly in a circle, tight and vast.
Vast is the prison I have cast.
Cast from the metal of my mind.
Mind is the trap I cannot find.
Find me the key to break the chain.
Chain is the thought, again, again.

Again the thought begins inside the quiet.

# 11. Small Altar

Do you want to know
what happiness is?

It's the weight of the cat when he sleeps on your chest,
a warm, purring anchor through all of the rest.
It's the first sip of coffee, that bitter, dark steam
That tells your tired brain it's okay to just dream.

It's finding a song you'd forgotten you loved,
and turning the volume up just because.
It's the smell of the rain on hot pavement at noon.
It's finishing a page, and not a moment too soon.

It's the clean, quiet sheet at the end of a long day.
It's having nothing important left to say.
It's not in the grand things, the fireworks and such.
It's in these tiny moments that don't ask for much.

They are small, quiet altars
where my spirit can rest.
And honestly?
I think they're the best.

# 12. The Tenant

The motor in the mattress hums a low, magnetic hymn.
My will, a sputtering pilot light, grows desperately dim.
These hands, these heavy anchors, are on loan from
someone else,
While I, the silent tenant, watch from hollowed-out
shelves.

The world is a bright, flat river beyond a pane of glass,
A silent, frantic broadcast on a never-ending pass.
My thumb, a rusty piston, scrolls the endless, burning
reel,
Consuming phantom tragedies, it simply cannot feel.
It's not a choice, this ritual; it is a draining charge,
A slow and steady freezing in a cold and concrete barge.

Then, the system jolts. A command from a distant, dusty
room.
A script to make the body rise and cross the waking
gloom.
The gears engage, a stiff, slow grind of bone and
weighted thread,
A marionette with fraying strings, pulled upward from
the bed.

And in the hall, the light is a blunt and clinical blade.
It dissects the morning, a thing of stark routine remade.
I watch the hands move, pour the water, perform the simple task,
From a million miles away, behind a one-way, tinted glass.
There is no memory of the motion, no echo of the thought,
Just the ghost of an instruction that the machinery was taught.

A presence in the cockpit, strapped in a plush and silent chair,
Eyes on the blinking console, breathing the processed air.
I see the data flowing, I know the ship's design,
But the connection to the helm is lost, a severed, tangled line.

So the body walks its pre-set paths, a vessel, cold and clean,
And I am just the static in the spaces in between.
A quiet, tranquil witness, numb and floating, bound to drift,
Watching my own life play out, a slow, perpetual gift.

# 13. Glimpse Inside the Noodle Sky

The flimble-wark of zizzer-zoof
Seeps through cracks in the spoon-proof roof.
A grommet spins its plastic joy,
While gnorts devour the tinfoil toy.

The shanklet moors with silent cleats,
On shores of fractured, sugar-beats.
And every zarg, with painted grin,
Collects the pins we're nested in.

The fribble-gust denies the bone,
The static hums a monotone.
We polish our reflective sneeze,
And bargain with the fangle-geese.

For in the zank, the stark, the true,
The goo defines what sticks to you.
The wobble-core, without a sound,
Is all the ground we've ever found.

# 14. The Wibble-Gahn Does Not Align

The sproingus in its flem-rack sleeps,
On pillows made of shattered sweeps.
A glorp-hahn whispers "zank" to "zood",
But finds the pibble-pank unglued.

The flidge has no more spangles left,
The frink is croodled, core-bereft.
A plonk-ghost taps its glassy tune,
On windows of a broken moon.

The skritchet mourns its missing "why",
The blip-scroll feeds on empty eye.
The gromble-flesh, a map of knots,
Remembers all the "ifs" and "whats."

The spangle-trip, a road of glue,
The yonk-god asks for something new.
But in the wibble-gahn's design,
No "then" can meet a "now" to twine.

The plink is dry. The vord has fled.
The snorf-locks cluster in my head.
They build a city with no name,
And whisper, "You are not to blame."

The grizzel-beam just hums and bends,
A message that it never sends.
The wohgt-words pile like phantom bone,
A kingdom built for me alone.

# 15. The Fribble-Gust at Noon

The fribble-gust denied the bone,
and left me feeling all alone.
It whispered through my wibble-gahn,
a dry and philosophical song.

The zizzer-zoof of thought took flight,
a frantic, fuzzy, fading light.
I tried to flimble with the latch,
But my own hands were a poor match.

The gronk-sphere rolled beneath the chair,
a perfect, polished sphere of care.
I could not reach it, could not throw,
Its silent, simple, spinning show.

The day was lost to pibble-pank,
a soggy, unfulfilled, grey blank.
And all my snorf-locks clustered tight,
and hummed me through the fading light.

# 16. The Plink is Dry

The plink is dry. The skingle snaps.
My yorr has curled and taken naps.
The fribble-gust denies the glarf,
and draws a wibble-gahn on my behalf.

A snorf-lock hums a dizzy-mote,
a stuck and sticky, single note.
It tangles with the gronk-sphere's gleam
and drowns it in a glorp-hahn's dream.

The flidge has lost its spangle-trip,
and sipped the last zizzer-zip.
The grizzel-beam just bends and ends,
A message for a zank it never sends.

So I will wait here, croodled deep,
where blip-scrolls feed and plonk-ghosts sleep.
And hope a flimble-wark will start,
and spin a new glimpse in my heart.

# 17. The Lay of the Wobble-Core

In the age of the Fribble-Gust,
before the Plink had gone to rust,
The Yonk-God yawned upon its Flem-Rack,
and spun the Zizzer-Zoof from black.

It took the Goo, the primal clay,
and formed a Gronk-Sphere to display.
It set a Wobble-Core inside,
where all the truth and tremors hide.

It gave it Snorf-Locks for its hair,
a nest of thought and tender care.
It gave a Grizzel-Beam for sight,
to bend the Zank and seek the light.

It set the Gromble-Flesh beneath,
a map of nerves, a tender wreath.
Then sent it on a Spangle-Trip,
with laughter on its Zizzer-Zip.

But oh, the path was Pibble-Pank,
the future made of brittle blank.
The Glorp-Hahn rose, a swallowing dread,

and filled the Misfit's heart with lead.

The Fangle-Geese began their honking deals,
As Gnorts arrived to chew its heels.
A Plonk-Ghost whispered of a brighter day,
now faded to a Dizzy-Mote's sad play.

Its Flidge grew weak, its Skingle snapped,
Its Yorr grew cold, its spirit mapped.
It tried to Flimble with a Shanklet's might,
but could not moor its hope aright.

It saw the Zargs, with painted glee,
collect the pins that held its knee.
It felt the Blip-Scroll's draining feed,
a Vord of sorrow, planted like a seed.

And so it Croodled, safe and small,
and heard the Wohgt-Words' silent call.
It felt the Sproingus in its chest,
a coiled, forgotten, joyful zest.

Then from the Wibble-Gahn's deep rift,
A Flimble-Wark bestowed a gift.
A Grommet spun, a perfect, simple key,
to set the tangled, weary spirit free.

It touched the Gronk-Sphere of its care
and found its Wobble-Core still there.
Though everything was strange and grand,
it understood its own Misfit land.

For in the Zank, the stark and true,
the Goo that sticks is you, just you.
So let the Fribble-Gust blow past,
your Wobble-Core is built to last

# 18. Glossary for a Misfit Mind

Plink (n.):
The smallest unit of creative thought or will.
A single, motivating, liquid drop, until
the well runs dry, the plink is gone,
And motivation can't be drawn.

Skingle (n.):
The thin, bright thread of a single, happy thought.
When it snaps, the joy you felt is come to naught.

Yorr (n.):
The core of inner warmth, a personal, quiet sun.
When it curls to sleep, all action comes undone.

Glarf (n.):
The raw, unshaped material for a dream or plan.
The courage and the hope to start, for any woman or
man.

Dizzy-mote (n.):
A single, looping, anxious thought that will not go.
A stuck and spinning record of a psychic woe.

Glorp-hahn (n.):
A heavy, swallowing feeling of profound despair.
The sense that you are sinking in the thick and static air.

Flidge (n.):
The inner mechanism, the will to start a task.
The engine of intention, that's all you need to ask.

Spangle-trip (n.):
The joyful, sparkling journey of a mind that's running free.
A happy, aimless mental exploration, you see.

Zizzer-zip (n.):
The electric, joyful energy of a brand-new, brilliant notion.
The vibrant, buzzing fuel for any mental motion.

Zank (n.):
The stark and heavy, simple, unadorned, and final truth.
The knowledge that arrives upon you, long after youth.

Croodled (adj.):
Curled inward, safe and hidden, in a defensive, private ball.
Protected from the world outside, and heeding no one's call.

Blip-scroll (n.):

The endless, draining feed of other people's lives and thoughts.

The river of comparisons in which your spirit rots.

Plonk-ghost (n.):

The hollow, echoing memory of a happiness that's passed.

A joy that's gone, whose shadow on the wall is cast.

Flimble-wark (n.):

The strange, productive magic of a mind that's working right.

The spark that cuts through static in the middle of the night.

Glimpse (n.):

A sudden, fleeting vision of a world that's whole and true.

A moment of connection, meant for only you.

# 19. Misfit Glossary Vol. II

Flimble (v.):
To move a hand that isn't yours, to wear another's skin.
To watch your own life happening, without being
within.

Zizzer-zoof (n.):
The phosphorescent residue of thoughts you can't quite
hold.
A background hum of maybe that never grows too old.

Grommet (n.):
A simple, plastic pivot on which simple joys may spin.
A perfect, tiny universe you find your peace within.

Gnorts (n.):
The silent, unseen munchers of your precious, quiet time.
The gnawing, small distractions that make reason hard to
climb.

Shanklet (n.):
A half-formed, shy intention that is moored before it's
free.
A hope that's tied securely to what you can never be.

Zarg (n.):
A painted, grinning figure that collects what you let fall.
The keeper of the little pins you're nested in, and all.

Fangle-geese (n.):
The honking, frantic bargains that your mind will make
for peace.
The deals you strike with silence to make all the static
cease.

Goo (n.):
The sticky, primal substance of what's real and what is
true.
The stuff that really makes you stick to everything you
do.

Wobble-core (n.):
The central, shaky axis on which all your turning spins.
The truth of you that trembles when the outer tumult
begins.

Sproingus (n.):
The coiled, potential energy for a forgotten, silly leap.
A joy that's packed in tension, buried deep in mental
sleep.

Flem-rack (n.):

The strange and weary furniture of a tired, troubled head.

Where odd and heavy feelings go to make their musty bed.

Pibble-pank (n.):

The feeling of a path ahead that's turned to brittle glue.

A future that's uncertain, soggy, and impossible to trek through.

Skritchet (n.):

The part of you that scratches at the door of a closed "why?"

The creature of inquiry that never seems to die.

Gromble-flesh (n.):

The living, breathing map of every worry and what-if.

A tapestry of knots and nerves, a tangled, tender glyph.

Yonk-god (n.):

The petty, inner deity of wanting something new.

That begs for a distraction, for a different, fresher view.

Vord (n.):

The perfect, platonic word-shape that exists before the sound.

The ghost of meaning on your tongue, forever being found.

Wohgt-words (n.):
The heavy, silent vocabulary of the things you'll never say.
A library of phantom books that slowly fade away.

# 20. Spectrum of Static

The core emits not light, but a chronic, low-grade want,
a Bose-Einstein condensate of things it does or don't.
Its signature is glitch tonic, always arriving before it's sent,
a negative kelvin comfort in a state of permanent dissent.
The waveform, when observed, collapses to a solid maybe,
a quantum superposition of "I can" and "I'm not able."

The central organ operates on sorrow-cycle deceit,
with efficiency approaching absolute zero heat.
It burns the fuel of almost and what could have been,
exhausting pure potentiality, again and again.
Its melancholy decreases, which defies the second law,
as it builds perfect, impossible memories from a single, fleeting flaw.

The social battery possesses a non-integer charge
and discharges in fractal patterns, both minute and large.
It resonates not with voices, but with the silent hum
of the background anxiety of the cosmos, a deafening glum.

Its impedance is imaginary, a root of negative grief,
shielding the core from a much-needed, belief-shattering
relief.

The internal chronometer ticks in looped time,
where the future is a memory, and past tense a charade.
It warps the local metric, creating a gravity well of why,
from which no photon of reason can ever fly.
The narrative is a Klein bottle, a one-sided, endless
surface,
containing a universe of proof, yet offering no purpose.

The spectrum is a lie, a consensual hallucination.
The subject is a phantom in its own self-observation.
All readings indicate a consciousness in a static state,
defined more by its absences than any tangible weight.
The final diagnosis, written in the data's cruel expanse:
A beautifully flawed experiment, given no second
chance.

# 21. The Architect

My mind is a bad architect.
It builds rooms with no doors.
It designs a house where the walls grow thorns.
And the welcome mat says, "Abandon all hope!"

It lays a foundation of "what if" and "should"
pours concrete made of my worst childhood fears
then looks at the blueprints and says, "This is good,"
while I've been living here for years.

I am the tenant. I am the ghost.
Paying rent in panic, I'm paying the cost.
Trying to hang a picture on a wall that won't hold it!
Trying to find a light switch in a socket that's blown it!

This mind, this architect, it's a sabotage artist!
It installs a fire alarm that screams when it's silent.
It builds a beautiful view, then nails the boards over it.
It points at the cracks and says, "*You're* the one that
caused it!"

So I walk these hallways, this prison of my design.
Kicking at the supports, trying to make the whole thing
collapse.

But the architect just whispers from a room in the back
of my mind,
"Don't you dare. This house is all you have."

This house is all you have.
This faulty house is all you have.
Don't test it in your style.

## 22. Weary Mind

The clock ticks out a warning,
It's half-past three,
And every single thought is a ship lost at sea.
That thing you said last Tuesday,
A look I can't define,
Makes my brain all tangled,
just like a fishing line.

Hush now, these thoughts are leaves in a stream,
Let me go, it's all just a dream.
The monster in my corner is a shadow on the wall,
Just breathe in, and breathe out, and let the quiet fall.

The night was never a blanket.
I wished the silence to be a friend
This may not be the beginning
But I'll let it be the end.
So, close your eyes, weary mind,
Let thy worries part,
Think of it another day,
Let me have a fresh start.

# 23. Glitch

The rain falls straight down.
The streetlights hum their one-note song.
A cat crosses the street, left to right.
A cat crosses the street, left to right.
The pattern is stable. The code is strong.

I check the time on my phone. 11:07 PM.
I walk past the bakery, its ovens cool and dark.
A man in a blue coat walks by, talking softly.
*A man in a blew coat walks by, talking softly.*
I blink. The world resets its mark.

My key turns in the lock. A familiar, grinding sound.
I hang my coat on the hook, on the hook, on the hook.
The silence in my apartment has a different texture now.
It feels like waiting for a question the universe forgot to allow.

Everything is fine. Everything is in its place.
Everything is fine. Everything is in its pl ace.
I pour a glass of water. The liquid is clear and wet.
I think I saw a pixel flicker, but I'm probably wrong.
I'm probably wrong.
I'm probably

i'm
I
i

.

# 24. The Fault Line

I watch them from the shoreline, their easy, tangled groups,
a forest growing thick and loud, with deep, entwined roots.
Their laughter is a language that I practice in my sleep,
a simple, fluent dialect my own voice cannot keep.

I am not an island; I have built my bridges, strong and true.
I have offered up my coordinates. I have sailed to them, and they to you.
For a season, there is landing. For a moment, there is port.
A shared and sheltered harbor, a comforting report.

Then, the tide pulls out. The silence is a subtle, growing stain.
The messages grow shorter, like a cord pulled from the brain.
No drama, no final earthquake, no slamming and shaking door,
just the quiet, glacial drifting from a receding shore.

And I am left with satellite images of where the
connection broke,
replaying all the conversations, like a cruel, forensic
joke.
Was it something in my frequency? A hum, a constant,
low-grade static?
A wavelength set to a private grief, a signal too erratic?

The groups reform like constellations, their patterns
fixed and bright,
while I am the rogue comet, burning out alone in the
night.
And the question is not why they left, but what is built
inside of me
That makes a home a temporary stay, and a friend a
memory?

Is there a flaw in my foundation, a crack in the design,
that turns all rooted, growing things into a passing,
borrowed vine?
I scan the faces in the hall, a ghost at my own feast,
and wonder if I am the reason that the connections have
been released.

# 25. Ghost Limb

We always feel the ghost limb.

You know the lore.
The sailor on solid ground who sways with the memory
of the sea.
The veteran whose fingers twitch for a glass that
shattered long ago.
That phantom echo.
That's the key.

It is a fist of fog,
clenched around the ghost of a bone,
sending sirens down a road that leads to a bridge long
since blown.
I spend my days trying to knead a knot from a muscle of
mist.
Hissing release.
Begging desist.

People see the surface, the unbroken skin.
They see ten fingers, a hand that can grip.
They preach, "Just lift the pen. Just grasp the door. Just
make the trip."

And I stare at this arm, this perfectly sculpted, working
limb...
and feel the searing spasm of what is not there.
An absence with a presence, a scream in the air.

It is the itch you cannot locate,
Because the chart is a fraud.
The map promises gold where the land has been sold,
and you're just carving canyons in your own flesh,
howling, "It burns, but it doesn't exist."

This is no alibi.
This is a border war on a map I did not draw.
One half of me hoists a white flag, pleads for a truce, for
a thaw.
The other is the ghost limb, a spectral command,
an army of echoes with static for hands.

So if you catch me gazing at my own palm,
testing its truth, feeling for a calm...
Do not tell me the battle is only a thought in my head.

I know.
That is the brutal, core-deep curse.
The ghost is in the machine,
and the machine... is the universe.

# 26. Whistle of the Kettle

You ask me what it's like, this constant, quiet dread?
It's the old kettle singing songs inside my head.

Not a modern marvel, quiet, sleek, and new,
but a relic, worn and weary, chipped in faded blue.
The kind that holds the memory of a thousand morning suns,
a vessel weighed with history on which my world now runs.

And from the moment consciousness begins to softly gleam,
some unseen hand has lit a fire, it seems, beneath my dream.

At first, a gentle hissing, a low and thrumming sound,
a tremor you could mistake for life, for purpose, safe and sound.
The tiny beads of *did I forget?* and *should I be afraid?*
They cling like liquid mercury, a price that must be paid.
That is the quiet overture, the music of the low...
the prelude to the rising heat that only I can know.

But the burner never cools off; the flame, it never dies,
It's fed by leaking pipelines of compromise and lies.
Of deadlines and of daydreams that curdle and go sour,
and the ghosts of conversations I replay by the hour.

So the hiss becomes a rattle, a shudder in my core.
The bubbles start their riot; they boil and beg for more.
They're *"you are not enough, you know,"* and *"see how fast they go?"*
A tempest in a teapot, a internal, growing woe.

I feel the steam's insistence, a pressure in my chest,
a silent, screaming aria that will not let me rest.
My very frame is humming, a note held sharp and long,
I am a captive instrument, a composer of the wrong.
And all the world just sees the pot, a simple, static sight,
and never sees the blazing ring, the ever-burning light.

And then... the whistle.
Not a choice, but a decree.
A simple, brutal law of thermal energy.
It is the sharp and sudden word, the tear you cannot bite,
the tremor in the cereal aisle that shatters the calm night.
A single, silver, scalding note, a final, frantic plea;
The only way the pressure knows to beg to be set free.

And people startle, react, they move me from the heat.
They solve the sound of suffering, a temporary feat.
But the flame?
Oh, the flame remains, a constant, hungry friend.
And the water in my belly has no cool, no quiet end.
And the cycle starts its rhythm, a rhythm I know well...
a hiss, a hum, a building scream, a slow, familiar hell.

So when I seem too quiet, when I am sitting still,
know I am fighting fire, with a formidable will.
I am taming all the tempests that in my belly steam,
just to keep from unleashing that final, piercing scream.

# 27. Blueprint for a Ghost

I keep the blueprint of your daughter taped inside my skull.
I trace its clean, predictable lines until my vision blurs.
A schematic for a soul: the right-angled smiles, the quiet, humming grace,
a mind that ticks in perfect time, that knows and keeps its place.
I have memorized the part. I know the lines I'm meant to speak.
So why is my throat filled with static, with a language that is weak?

God, I wish my brain were built from brick and simple, solid things;
from discipline and focus, and the peace that routine brings.
Instead, it's a shattered mirror-hall, a frantic, buzzing hive,
a thousand different channels screaming, none of them alive.
It's a radio that picks up every station but the one I need,
a garden choked with glorious, chaotic, useless weed.

I see the quiet disappointment in the language of your sigh,

The way you gently ask again, "You didn't even try?"

And I want to scream, "I TRIED UNTIL MY SYNAPSES WORE THIN!

I fought a civil war inside the fortress of my skin!

I carved out hours and offered them upon that altar, 'Study,'

But my thoughts were just a swarm of flies, a frantic, bloody, muddy."


I would break my own bones to rebuild them in the shape you recognize.

I would sand the strange grain from my heart, I would pluck the strange dreams from my eyes.

I would silence every weird and wandering note my spirit sings,

to be the simple, solid, easy daughter that your love deserves.

But this creature that I am is stubborn, it is rooted deep and wild,

this misfit heart, this frantic mind, your brilliant, broken child.

And the greatest, ugliest truth that claws its way up from the deep

is the furious, helpless knowledge that I can't make you proud before I go to sleep.

That the cost of my existence is a pain I didn't mean to make,

a permanent, quiet failure for a tired parent's sake.

So I wear the name of disappointment like a crown of lead,

the daughter of the blueprint, but a different child instead.

# 28. Non-Aggression Treaty

Alright, listen up, you vast, dramatic Space,
Wipe that look off your infinite, endless face.
We've been doing this dance for a number of years,
And it's giving me headaches, it's feeding my fears.
So let's sign a treaty, you and me, right here,
To make our co-existence a bit more clear.

Article the First:
You agree to stop whispering, post-midnight, "You're alone,"
And I will stop throwing my socks at your general tone.
Your existential dread is a tired, old bit,
And frankly, your timing is never a hit.

Article the Second:
You may keep the dark matter, the black holes, the void,
But my last slice of pizza cannot be destroyed.
That is a boundary, a line in the sand,
The most sacred of laws in this whole mortal land.

Article the Third:
When I'm feeling quite happy and bubbling with cheer,
You are not to appear with a "But why are you here?"
No cosmic reminders that "all dust returns,"

While I'm trying to master a difficult turn.

Article the Fourth:
In return, I concede, on the second Tuesday of each moon,
I will ponder my insignificance, preferably past noon.
I'll grant you one hour of pure, frantic dread,
Then I'm watching some cat videos, going to bed.

Article the Fifth:
You stop claiming my keys, my phone, and my will,
And I'll admit that your silence is sometimes a thrill.
That the nothing you offer can, strangely, make room
For a new kind of something to quietly bloom.

So we sign it in starlight, we seal it with grace,
You, the great, hungry Nothing, and me, in my place.
You stick to the cosmos, I'll stick to the ground,
And we'll both stop pretending the other's profound.

A truce with the Void! What a hilarious thought!
...Wait, where are my books? This treaty is naught!
You tricked me, you monster! You vast, empty fraud!
...
...
...Ah, forget it. It's fine. We're still pretty odd

# 29. System Rest

The frozen blue screen, a cold and static sea,
A wheel that spins for an eternity.
A ghost trapped within the machine's cold light,
Holding its breath through the endless night.

I press the power with a silent, pleading prayer,
A ritual performed in the stagnant air.
A count of ten, a hope to be unbound,
To finally hear a welcome, booting sound.

The fan whirs to life, a soft and steady hum,
A gentle promise that the calm has come.
The icons bloom like flowers in the dawn,
The lonely, haunting ghost inside is gone.
The world is waiting, patient and the same,
And for a fleeting moment, I remember my own name.

# 30. A Week for a Wandering Soul

Monday's Mandate:

Polish all the silence till the surface is a sheet of glass.
Return the borrowed echo to the hollow, empty past.
Teach the tired clock to make the morning hours last.
Learn the definition of a shadow you have cast.

Tuesday's To-Dos:

Reconcile the distance from a memory to a star.
Find the missing moon; you can't have lost it very far.
Water all the plastic plants and name them where they
are.
Mend the broken frequency that picks up from afar.

Wednesday's Work:

Remember how to be a solid, weighted, real thing.
Practice how to let the solid to the breezes bring.
Translate the cat's slow purring to the song the sirens
sing.
Untangle all the knots that in your neural threads now
cling.

Thursday's Tasks:

Debug the dream of airports where the flights are never
led.
Build a nest from all the kind and unanswered things
you've said.
Digitize the childhood of the ghost inside your head.
Paint the setting sun a different, less familiar red.

Friday's Final Calls:

Achieve a steady orbit, or just sort the socks instead.
For the galaxy is in the laundry, and the universe's in
your head.
Determine if you are the user, or a thought the system
bred.
Then forget the question utterly, and just go back to bed.

# 31. Catechism of the Ruin

You are the scripture I should never have read.
A gospel of hands, and a thorny, wild bed.
You built an altar inside of my chest,
And I, the willing fool, gave you the rest.
I canonized your shadows, I blessed all your flaws,
And drank the sweet poison, ignoring the cause.

Loving you was like holding a blade by the sharpest part,
A beautiful violence that tore me apart.
I collected the scars like they were holy degrees,
And I knelt in the wreckage, pretending to please.
You were the fire, and I was the moth,
Whispering "Burn me," my unspoken oath.

I built you a city behind my own eyes,
A kingdom for you, a forlorn, desperate prize.
I painted the sky with the blue of your name,
And let all my other stars die out in the flame.
You were the storm I called "home," the chaotic, loud sea,
And I was the shoreline, erased willingly.

Now the fever has broken. The saint has been cast
From the cathedral he built from my future and past.
The hymns are all silent. The pews are all dust.

In the ruins, a different, more resilient trust.
I am gathering the pieces you never thought I would
find,
The ones that were purely, entirely mine.

So take your sainthood. Take your dark, twisted crown.
This temple is crumbling, I'm tearing it down.
I am learning the prayer of my own beating heart,
A liturgy written for a brand-new, solitary start.
I was your ruin. You were my prayer.
And now, I am the answer, standing right here.

# 32. What is Madness?

Madness is grown-ups talking in low, rumbling tones.
It's the jumping of the house when they slam the doors.
It's the monster you *know* is in the closet,
and the terrible, confusing quiet when they say it isn't
spotted.
It is a feeling with no name, a storm in a room with no
windows.

Madness is wearing yellow and orange on a Tuesday.
It is laughing too loud in a silent hallway.
It is the boy who writes poems about the cracks in the
pavement.
It is caring *so much* about a band, a book, a look,
that your heart feels like it will either crystallize or
combust.
It is the terrifying, brilliant madness of a soul building its
own skeleton.

Madness is staying up until 3 a.m. to build a life on a
screen.
It is the quiet, creeping dread that you are forever
behind.
It is the calculated risk, the maxed-out credit card of the
soul to find.

It is the terrifying freedom of a map with no destination,
and the thought you weren't given those secret
instructions,
raising a sense of gnawing suspicion.


Madness is the silent scream in the grocery store aisle.
It is the suffocating order of a perfectly made bed, all
pristine.
It is the relentless, ticking meter of productivity.
It is the quiet, systematic dismantling of your own
dreams
to pay the mortgage on a life
you no longer recognize.
Madness is not chaos.
It is the price of stability.


Madness is the quiet.
It is the way the names of your old friends slip away like
smoke.
It is watching the world you built become a relic, a
museum show.
It is the young, with their frantic, buzzing energy,
for remembering a slower, softer world, calling *you*
crazy.
Madness is not losing your mind.
It is watching the world lose its soul.

Madness is the single, fixed point in a world of
compromise.
It is the vision that will not let you sleep.
It is the burden of a truth no one else can bear to see.
They call it obsession.
I call it duty.
A sane person would have given up.
My madness is what saves you.

Madness is creating a new world
because you saw the old one was rotten.
It is order, perfect and terrible,
born from the ashes of their chaos so foreign.
They call me mad because my love for a better future is a
consuming fire.
Their madness is their sentimentality.
Their attachment to broken things.
I am not mad.
I am the only one who is truly, terrifyingly sane.

# 33. Always Your Fault

Of course, it was your fault.
You should have known what "yes" was,
a different definition in their hands.
It never means "yes."
It means "yes, and also tomorrow,
and next week, and your entire spine."

It was totally your fault.
For not being a mind-reader,
for not knowing that "be happy" actually meant
"disappear into a smiling, silent, convenient ghost
who anticipates our every need before we even feel it."

Of course, it was your fault.
You breathed wrong.
You existed in a room with too much oxygen,
and didn't apologize for stealing their air.
You had a bad day on a day they needed a mirror,
and your crack in the glass ruined their reflection.

It was absolutely your fault
For thinking your "no"
was a word they had in their vocabulary.
You handed them a boundary like it was a gift,

and they treated it like a bomb that needed defusing
by handing it right back to you, now ticking louder.

So yes. It was your fault.
For having a heart that wasn't bulletproof.
For having a "help me" that was louder than your "I'm
fine."
For being a person instead of a painting on their wall.

It was all your fault.
And it will always be your fault
until the day you stop existing in their lives.

# 34. The Border

I remember the exact shade of blue of the sky that day.

*I remember the weight of the lie you were about to say.*

It was cerulean, a painter's color, pure and clean.

*It was the color of a deep and cold, and unforgiving sea.*

We stood on the shore, and you promised me forever.

*We stood on the shore, and I knew I was clever.*

Your hand in mine felt like a final, solid truth.

*Your hand in mine was just a tactic of my youth.*

I built a city of our memories, with towers tall and bright.

*I was the demolition expert, working through the night.*

I can still hear the echo of your laughter in the hall.

*I can still feel the thrill of watching your foundations fall.*

Why did you do it? Was our love not enough?

*Love was the weapon. And I loved watching you break.*

I will never forgive you.

*I will never need you to.*

# 35. Stay

okay. alright. I get it, you know?
You don't have to do this all for show,
I understand, and I want to learn.
But you need to tell me what I have to earn.
It's not fine. But it's alright.
And I need to know that you'll keep fighting this fight.
Maybe I should have done more,
or maybe you need to stop being so sure
I get it. you want to try to be 'normal'.
But does anyone understand what's in their own
journal?

I understand. I'll say it again.
I'll shut up because no one gets it.
I'll shout because you need to hear this.
And I won't give up until you push me out
I won't stop until you stop the doubt.
I'll apologize for what they did
Or I'll ignore the part where you hid.
But please, oh please, don't disappear from me
I need you now, and you've always been my dream.

# 36. Down Below

Down, down below.
That's where he was.
Down below, where there was no snow

where the light had reached, low and slow
where the road stretched on more and more
where the night was dark yet bright at the door
where the memory was old but still with a core
where the Saturday bells never rang without chores
where the Monday morning had a lucky horse
where the TV static buzzed in Morse.
And the code was a melody stuck in loss
And the wonder was his curiosity's boss
And the 'maybe' and the 'should be' were just a cause
And they weren't children of the jobs
Where the lady in red never had many stops
where the old man always was wearing bronze
And the kids in the woods always knew the response
And the box and the tops and the palms and the bombs
And the stupid white sheets with lines in the halls
were there but not present
Never ruling their life.
Never owning their will
and their love and their might.

And maybe, just maybe, that's what it was.
Maybe he knew what his purpose was.

Down, down below.
Because that's where he was.
He was down there where there was no snow.

# 37. Days

It's been a year
Or two. Maybe five
It's been a while
And I don't know how many miles.
The days go by
Miniscule, unimportant.
Everything is scheduled.
But don't know where I lost it.
I'm looking for it hard
All day and night.
What is it I'll find is a mystery I'll unwind.
I can't fathom the thought.
I can't breathe the lies.
I can't forgive or forget.
I can't stand here blind.

It's not me
It's not them
It's not us
It's not here
Was it there when I first learned this cheer?
Were we looking for you all loud and clear?
Or was this another way to impale a spear?

It's alright.
I'll find it someday,
or maybe I'll forget as usual, it's okay!
I don't know what you are.
I don't know what you want.
But I need to find you.
Maybe just to taunt.

# 38. Lost Frequencies

I am the curator of a museum of the gone,
where the only exhibits are waves that have moved on.
My first great relic is a digital, chittering screech,
the modem's bold anthem, a song just out of reach,
that heralded a world through a wire, thin and new.
Now, its unique static is a ghost in the blue.

Then, the tenor of an engine, a specific, rumbling purr
from a red car's heart, a defining, family stir.
The thud of its door was a period, a solid, certain sound,
on the sentence of an evening, when our world was
small and bound.

I have the scuff and thud of a pair of worn-out boots,
kicking through gravel, dismissing all disputes.
The crystalline shimmer, the rustle of a gown,
my mother's own magic, before she put it down.

The constant, low whirring, a comforting, warm breath,
from the family laptop, humming life against death.
The chorus of kittens, behind the house, a tiny, pleading
cry,
and the sound of the sunlight, flittering through clouds
in a boundless, old sky.

But my collection expands past the borders of me,
to a world growing quieter, as you'll plainly see.
The calm of the road, a low, whispered rush,
is now just a blaring, a metallic, harsh crush.

The wind-chimes that gossiped in tinny, bright prose,
have fallen to silence, their melodies froze.
The buzzing of bees, that thick, golden sound,
is a rarity now on the hallowed, green ground.

The crickets' clockwork, that stitching of night,
is forever hidden, erased from the light.
And the call of the peacock, that rain-promising wail,
is a story now silenced by a different, sad gale.

So I walk through my halls, in the quiet of my mind,
and I play back the echoes that the world left behind.
For every lost frequency, a memory is bound
in the silent, vast museum of the world's fading sound.

# 39. I Didn't Need You

I didn't need you.
It's not like my world got quiet and small,
Or that I noticed your absence, like a missing wall.
I just suddenly decided to become a hermit, you see,
And your silence just perfectly aligned with my new
philosophy.

I didn't need you.
We never were friends, not really, no way.
We just killed time together, filled up the day.
It's a total coincidence that all of the songs on the radio,
Are the ones that we screamed in the car, don't you
know?

I didn't need you.
I just had a sudden, profound revelation,
To delete all our photos from my whole damn vacation.
And that inside joke that still makes me smile?
I'm just practicing laughing. It'll take a while.

I didn't need you.
It's not like I'm haunted by things left unsaid.
I just talk to myself now, inside of my head.

And when I check my phone, it's not your name I hope
for,
I'm just deeply invested in my battery's percentage, that's
all.

I didn't need you.
My heart doesn't ache. It's just practicing chords.
It's not like I'm keeping some kind of sad score.
I'm doing just perfectly, couldn't be more at ease.
And if you ever come back?
...I didn't need you.
Whatever.

# 40. Bunker

Location: A quiet chamber, nestled in the mind.
Status: Everlasting, peaceful, and defined.

Walls: Woven from the fabric of a softer, simpler day.
Foundation: Built on games the years could not erase.
Lighting: From the glow of a forgotten cartoon's face.

Jars of firefly hope, lined up in a row.
Cans of quiet laughter from a long time ago.
The taste of birthday cake, the scent of summer rain.
A map of all the places where you learned to live with
pain.

A child lives here, made of butterfly wings and light,
Who never learned the meaning of a truly endless night.
She hums a tune of rainbows, simple, sweet, and clear,
The only constant occupant who has no room for fear.

From this silent, guarded, deeply personal space,
I see the inner children on each hurried face.
I see the knight, the scientist, the artist, and the shy,
The different, lovely costumes that they show to
passersby.

And though their games seem different, and their stories aren't the same,
The whispered wish they carry is a single, shared, true name:
A need to feel seen and held, to feel truly, deeply known,
A silent, desperate prayer that they do not voice alone.

So from my bunker, I send back a soft and steady sound,
A frequency for lost young things, on which this truth is found:
"I see the child you had to hide. I know your secret part.
You are forever safe and loved within this bunkered heart."

# 41. Just Let Go

In English, we say, 'let go of the past,'

But in poetry, we say,
It is not a balloon released into a blue, boundless sky.
It is pulling your own roots from a ground you called
home.
It is unstitching your name from a story you memorized
by heart,
and learning to wear the scar of its absence like a new,
unfamiliar art.

It is not a clean break, but a slow, cellular ache,
a quiet civil war for your own spirit's sake.
For the past is not a place you simply walk out of and
lock the door.
It is the very soil from which you are desperately trying
to grow more.

So we do not 'let go' as if it were a simple, graceful task.
We learn to hold the love, and stop wearing the mask
of the person we were in the wreckage and the glee.
We let go of the past to make room for the new 'me'.

# 42. Lost Signal

the router in the heart
blinks a steady, amber no.
a stalled and spinning wheel
where the feelings used to go.

searching for networks...
searching...
one bar of a forgotten song.
The password is incorrect.
The connection weakens.
Then is gone.

We are all just ghosts
in the machine of each other,
sending messages that fail to send.
Are you still there?
Please respond.
a love, grown brittle,
waiting for a signal to transcend.

The silence is a 404:
emotion not found.
I refresh the empty page.
The only sound

is the quiet hum
of a server, cooling down.

# 43. Silence the Engine

There is a place the maps ignore,
a fracture in the common core.
Where signals cross and meanings fray,
and solid things dissolve away.
A silent static, thick and deep,
where promises of order sleep.
I built my house on such a site,
a citizen of endless night.

Then, one day, a different sound,
a rhythm in the barren ground.
Not a voice, but more a pulse,
a subtle, atmospheric waltz.
I cupped my hands to catch the beat,
a fragile, almost-dying heat.
I gave it breath. I gave it form.
A shelter from the inner storm.

I am not building palaces of rhyme,
I am buying myself a little time.
With every metaphor I cast,
I am making a future that can last.
This is not some gentle art;
It's surgery upon the heart.

It is the tourniquet I tie
before that part of me can die.

The words are not my final plea,
they are the lock and they are the key.
They are the anchor and the chain,
the solace for a specific pain.
They do not scream, they do not cry,
they simply prove I have not died.
Upon this page, in silent ink,
is the air I need to think.

So when you see the finished, quiet page,
you witness the concluding stage
of a battle fought in silent, desperate rage.
A victory, not grand or sweet,
but the simple fact I did not meet
the darkness on its own bleak terms.
I built a world that safely turns.
You see a poem, neat and penned.
I see the bruise that finally mend.
I see the hand that held the knife,
and chose instead to carve a life.

# 44. Call It Rebellion

Maybe I'm selfish, a word they fling with scorn,
when I choose the path less trod, the self reborn.
I want to help myself first, to mend the cracks inside,
to find the strength where my own wounds reside.

But according to my society, it's a want, not a thirst,
a fleeting whim, a selfish seed that's cursed.
They preach devotion to the common good,
a selfless life, completely understood.

But what of the soul that's starving, unheard,
a silent plea, a whispered, desperate word?

I can't imagine how life would be,
if I only had thought about listening to me.
Would the constant battle cease the inner strife?
Would there be joy, a truer, vibrant life?
No longer swayed by voices from the crowd,
my own song rising, strong and clear and loud.

To honor instincts, whispers from my core,
to open doors I'd never seen before.
To choose my path, though others may not see,
the silent courage, the quiet victory.

To heal the self, to finally feel truly free,
a revolution sparked, just by listening to me.

# 45. Beckoning Horizon

I have lived and I have died,
a thousand silent deaths, a soul denied.
I have been here before, in the desolate space,
where shadows danced and left no trace.
But something shifts, a tremor in the core,
it feels like the only thing I want to do is explore.

These wonderful places, whispered on the breeze,
cities humming, ancient, sacred trees.
Mountains calling, oceans wide and deep,
secrets held where quiet rivers sleep.
A thirst awakens, unfamiliar, strong,
to step outside where I've belonged.
Only in sorrow, only in the night.
Now, the world beyond beckons with its light.

These wondrous people, their stories yet untold,
their laughter warm, their spirits brave and bold.
Faces I've not met, hands I've yet to hold,
a tapestry of life, vibrant and old.
No longer bound by what has been,
a new horizon, sharp and keen.
A whisper of adventure, a forgotten art,
a different rhythm for my waking heart.

Perhaps this time, I'll truly see,
the beauty waiting, just for me.

# 46. Weight That Returns

I'm here again, where I hoped I'd never be,
a chilling echo in this silent room,
a twisted knot of dread inside of me.
I'm here, and my heart wishes it to be a dream,
a nightmare's grip I cannot shake or flee,
each breath a struggle, a suffocated scream.

I'm floating, and I think I am scared,
adrift in absence, tethered to no shore.
The air is heavy, thick with what I've shared
with ghosts and shadows knocking at my door.
I'm staring, but I think my vision is impaired,
the edges blurred, the colors dull and gray,
a world refracted through a lens of despair.

My mind jumbled, perhaps I have a spare?
A different thought, a life I could have worn,
a joyful mind that's light beyond compare.
But this one's broken, weary and forlorn,
a shattered compass leading everywhere.
My fingers red, maybe from blood,
or perhaps the friction of a life worn thin,
but I couldn't bring myself to care.
The numbness settles, deep within my skin,

a quiet surrender to the rising flood.
I simply wait for where it pulls me in.

# 47. Silencing Echo

I watched as a leaf fell into the water,
but it wasn't me watching.
I felt like I was just another celestial being,
slowly being forgotten.

My head felt empty, my heart was sore,
I tried clawing my eyes open.
I could see light from under the door,
a faint glow, a distant token.

I tried to ask for help, to scream, to reach out,
but the silence in my head grew ever so loud.
A phantom whisper, a mocking scout,
wrapping me tighter in its shroud.

I was drowning in air, I watched my body burn,
a silent pyre, consuming my core.
I think a pair of hands are wrapped around my throat,
and I waited for the snap,
for it to be over as I stared.
I closed my eyes and silently asked to be read,
minutes went by, hours, maybe days,
maybe someone finally thought that I wasn't a waste,
that there was a seed of something worth saving, a

fragile trace.

I looked up to see my eyes staring back at me,
a reflection, a stranger, yet undeniably I.
She said it was time, her voice like a chilling decree,
as I told her to leave me be.

But her gaze held steady, a silent plea,
a mirror of the pain that resided in me.
"This is not your end," her presence seemed to say,
"There's still a sunrise after this endless gray."

A tremor ran through me, a faint, fragile spark,
as if a distant memory pierced the dark.
The hands on my throat loosened, the burning eased,
and a single, silent tear, at last, was released.

# 48. The Chamber

I've been stuck in a chamber.
A cave with a single, vicious voice
And it doesn't just whisper.
It shouts with a clamor.
It doesn't give you a choice.

It says, "They are talking."
*They are talking.*
"It's about you."
*It's about me.*
"And you came up short."
*I came up short.*
"And they all knew."
*And they all knew.*

I try to shout back! I try to scream "LIAR!"
But the walls are too close; they just throw it right back.
They throw it right back with a hissing, hot fire.
"Your voice is too quiet."
*My voice is too quiet.*
"Your logic is flawed."
*My logic is flawed.*
"Just sit down and be silent."
*Just sit down and be silent.*

This chamber, this prison, it has its own weather.
It's a hurricane made of my own recycled air.
It's me versus me, and we're tied together.
Screaming at a reflection that just doesn't care.

So if I seem breathless, if I seem distant and strange,
it's because I'm in that cave, rearranging the stones.
Trying to change the refrain, trying to alter the range
of the echo that lives in the marrow of my bones.

The echo that lives...
*(the echo that dies...)*
The echo that lives...
and always forgives...
The worst things I've ever said.

# 49. Overflowing Endlessness

I think the sun is broken.
It bleeds through the blinds like a drunk god's last
confession,
staining the walls the color of forgotten medicine.
I swallow the light. It tastes like a battery.

We built our cities from the bones of question marks,
stacked them high enough to puncture heaven's
underbelly.
Now the sky wheezes, a lung full of smog and satellites.
Progress is a noose woven from telephone wires.

I tried to care today.
Pressed my ear to a stranger's chest,
heard the ocean trapped in a plastic bottle.
They say we're advanced.
(Then why do we still apologize for bleeding?)

My reflection is a fossil in the toaster.
It screams when I press the lever down.
I laugh. Or maybe it's the sound of a chair
giving up beneath the weight of a man
who forgot how to stand.

The moral of the story?
The page is on fire.
The alphabet is running for its life.

# 50. Standardized Human Protocol

Welcome, new unit, to the finalized design.
Your purpose is simple: to function and shine.
Please follow this manual, this protocol divine,
To ensure your performance stays perfectly in line.

When you boot up each morning, with sleep in your
eyes,
Execute *'basic startup smile'* for the spies.
Then run a diagnostic, and to your surprise,
You'll find all your messy emotions are lies.

In social encounters, please follow the script,
A collection of phrases, pre-tested and tripped.
With calibrated eye-rolling and perfectly lipped,
Ensure every last shred of your soul has been stripped.

Your value is measured in output and gain,
In conquering tasks through frustration and strain.
If you ever feel motivation is on the wane,
Just run *'compare to peers'* to feel the shame rain.

Consume the required nutrients, but do not enjoy,
This body's a machine that you must employ.

Schedule downtime, your systems to deploy,
And be sure to mute every authentic noise of joy.

We've found several processes, useless and old,
Like *'wonder at raindrops'* and stories untold.
They'll be scrubbed from your core, and we're happy and
bold,
For a unit that's running efficiently is gold.

If you feel a strange hollowness deep in your core,
A sense that this life is a terrible chore,
Do not panic. It's a glitch, nothing more.
Just run the system scan, and ignore what it's for.

# 51. Fossil Record of a Sterile Mind

The Bedrock of Ignored Advice
We begin in the deep time, the primordial clay,
Where warnings like trilobites, fossilized, lay.
A stratum of "shoulds" and of "don'ts" and of "can'ts,"
The sedimentary weight of a thousand firm aunts.
Here, found in the shale, is a small, perfect tooth,
The first lie I told that I knew was the truth.
It shines in the light, a small, defiant white bone,
The first little seed of a self I would own.

The Petrified Forest of Youth
Above it, the ghost of a petrified wood,
Where feeling and logic once tangled and stood.
The air here is amber; it holds the faint sound
Of a name that I called my own hunting ground.
We've found a small dagger, carved out of a wish,
And the bowl of a skull that belonged to a fish.
A creature that swam in the depths of a dream,
Before the world taught me to follow the stream.
A cast of a footprint, too large for the frame,
Proof of the giant I hoped I'd become.

The Great Extinction Event
A layer of ash, universal and deep,
Where the slow, grazing dinosaurs of innocence sleep.
Here, skeletons huddle, the great, gentle beasts,
Unconditional trust, taken down by the least.
A carbonized feather of hope, turned to stone,
And the meteorite: a harsh word, spoken alone.
This is the boundary, the clear, brutal line,
Between a world that was yours, and a world that was
mine.

The Volcanic Rebirth
Then, chaos. A flow of sharp, volcanic glass,
The beautiful violence after the pass.
This rock is obsidian, sharp, and it gleams.
The product of pressure and subterranean screams.
Here, new minerals crystallized in the pain,
A diamond of resolve, forged in the rain.
A geode of silence, which, cracked open, shows
A cavern of crystals where no sunlight goes.

The River Delta of Now
And here is the surface, the present-day mud,
The silt of the everyday, the pulse of the blood.
We find modern artifacts, scattered and strange,
The detritus of living, arranged and rearranged.
A bottle-cap medal from a battle I lost,

A key with no lock, lightly covered in frost.
The fresh, fragile bones of a song half-remembered,
And the deep, twisting root of a love dismembered.

Conclusion of the Dig:
So this is the map of the fault lines and shifts,
A landscape constructed from fractures and drifts.
I am the site and the scientist, both.
Interpreting echoes, exhuming an oath.
Not a ruin to mourn, but a history, layered and true,
A testament written by all I've been through.
And the digging goes on, in the quiet and grime,
For the next fossil layer, the next part of time.

# 52. Following Footsteps

I'm being haunted in ways I can't understand.
seeing things that aren't there,
finding clothes I can't wear.
It's stupid and it's pointless
But it's a way to spice up life.

It's like I'm being followed.
My footsteps echo sound,
like they're walking right behind me,
silent yet too loud.
In a way, it's exhilarating.
The stress and mysteriousness,
but it's draining my insides,
This impure, scratched chess.

It wasnt always like this,
the faces in the dark,
the scents in the bark,
the moths playing their part,
leaving its permanent mark.

It's a game of cat and mouse.
But the cat is not the one you'll see,
The mouse isn't the one who'll breathe,

The chase isn't in an empty street,
The reward would be their scream, i'll dream.

# 53. Universal Translation Guide

When she says: "It's nothing, don't worry, it's fine."
It means: I've drawn a new border, an emotional line.
The "nothing"'s a canyon, too vast to cross yet,
And the subject is closed, so just pay the damn debt.

When she says: "Do whatever you want, I don't care."
It means: I am currently braiding my own deep despair.
This is a test you are destined to fail,
Now watch you walk straight into the jaws of this whale.

What I say: "Who's a good boy? Yes, you are!"
What it means: You are the one constant, my truest
north star.
Your love is a language with no word for "betrayal,"
You've saved me from sinking on most days with your
tail.

What I say: "Okay, I'm leaving! Be good now, you hear?"
What it means: My soul feels like I'm abandoning you,
my dear.
I'd rather sit here and forever be bored,
Than miss the pure welcome that you will afford.

What I say: "I'm doing fine, it's under control."
What it means: My mind is a burning, self-sustaining coal.
The architecture inside is a crumbling design,
And "under control" is a fictional, flimsy new line.

What I say: "I just need to lie down for a bit."
What it means: The engine is flooded, the spark plugs are lit.
My system's rebooting from critical overload,
And carrying this conversation is a desolate road.

Heaven says: "All souls can be saved through divine, loving grace."
It means: We're a bit short on quota, we need the space.
Your suffering is part of a beautiful plan,
Now stop asking questions and fall into line, man.

Hell says: "Abandon all hope, ye who enter here."
It means: Welcome, we're glad that you finally appear.
You'll find we're more honest, the management's sound,
And the hope you abandoned was never around.

So listen not just to the words that are said,
But the universe speaking inside of your head.
For the truest translation, the final, best clue,
Is often the silence that's speaking to you.

# 54. The Reluctant Host

I am the spine, the chalky, white tree,
The scaffold of bone that was forced to agree
To host this tempest, this luminous guest,
This frantic, wet star in my calcium nest.
My vertebrae stack, a reluctant ascent,
To the chaotic kingdom, the cerebrum has rent.

Above me, it crackles, a synaptic storm,
A universe building its own complex form.
It thinks its grand thoughts of love and of dread,
While I bear the weight of each word left unsaid.
The tension translates to a tangible ache,
A seismic complaint for the host's silent sake.

Oh, the brain is a wonder, I'll grudgingly attest,
A rainforest firing inside of the chest.
It paints with its chemicals, dopamine, serotonin,
A masterpiece bathed in a neurotic, bright light.
But its art has a cost, a metabolic price,
A demand for more sugar, a call to suffice.

And I am the road, the aorta's red rush,
The obedient river that answers the hush
Of a billion small neurons all screaming for fuel,

Playing servant and subject to this mental duel.
I flood it with oxygen, nutrients, and grief,
Carrying hope on the back of a leaf.

For the brain builds its castles of intangible things,
On the strength of my marrow, the pull of my strings.
It dreams of the cosmos, it writes its sad verse,
While I am the anchor, the blessing and curse.
The solid, dumb fact that it cannot outrun,
The ladder it climbed on to block out the sun.

So I stand here, a pillar of patient complaint,
A testament wrought without a saint.
Housing a galaxy, brilliant and vast,
In a structure of bone that was never built last.
I am the foundation, the reluctant, true host
Of the beautiful, terrible thing I fear most.

# 55. The Museum of Almost-Selves

First, know the Loom: the fabric of all that Is,
is woven from the thread of every single Was.
And every choice, a tremor in the cosmic hand,
unravels one bright strand to weave a different land.
For every path you walked, a billion paths were shorn,
and in that act of choosing, other yous were born.

Welcome. This hall is silent, save for phantom heartbeats'
sound.
Here, other versions of your soul on other Earths are
bound.
Each is a variation on the theme that makes you You,
a different permutation of the things you thought you
knew.

Behold, in Gallery One, behind a pane of crystal air:
**The You Who Did Not Overthink**, the you who did not
care
so deeply for the syntax of a stranger's glancing slight.
This one sleeps through the night, my dear. She does not
dread the night.
Her brow is smooth as morning, her laughter is a simple
bell.

(She has her own quiet sorrows, other versions of her hell.)

Here, in the Wing of Confidence, a figure, standing tall:
**The You Who Took the Microphone** and held a crowd in thrall.
Her voice does not turn inward to a chambered, echoing scream.
She wears her skin like victory; she lives within the dream.
She does not trace the fault lines in the architecture of her mind.
(But oh, the loneliness of being forever defined.)

And this one, in the Amber Room, where time has slowed to glass:
**The You Who Stayed and Built a Home** upon a plot of grass.
Her hands are in the garden's soil, her future is a tree.
A simpler, sweeter story than the one you had to flee.
She has the love you wondered of, the comfort of the known.
(She sometimes stares at passing jets and feels completely alone.)

I see you seek the darkest hall, the one you fear the most.
**The You Who Shattered Utterly**, the one whom hope let go.
She is not framed in gold, but in the shadows that she braves.
She is the proof of your own strength, the life your courage saves.
For she is the contingency, the path you walked beside.
The one you are still fighting, with her still alive inside.

So do not mourn these almost-selves, these ghosts in crystal tombs.
They are not failures, they are not your could-have-been dooms.
They are the cosmic evidence of your own agency,
the map of every battle, the "what if" and "let be."
You are the sum of every path your soul was brave to take,
the living, breathing artifact of every single break.

You are the curator here. The main exhibit, whole and true.
The universe that chose to be, magnificently, you.

# 56. Tabs

My mind is a browser with fifty-six tabs open.
Fifty-six windows to a world I can't close.

Tab one is a weather report for a city I left.
Tab two is a recipe for a cake I'll never bake.
Tab three is a silent, black screen where I replay
a conversation from 2019, searching for a mistake.

Tab twelve is a PDF of a chapter from ninth grade.
The one about mitochondria, lost and unread.
Tab seventeen is a photo of a top I wore when I was five,
It's polka dots forever imprinted in my mind.

Tab twenty-four is a live feed of a family trip from last
year,
the feeling of the sun on my neck, a laughter I can
almost hear.
Tab thirty-three is a blank document, titled "What You
Should Have Said."
Its cursor blinking mockingly, a thought forever unshed.

And then there are the critics.
Tab forty-one is a running commentary on my posture.
Tab forty-five is a list of every time I laughed too loud.

Tab forty-eight is a live transcript, correcting my grammar in real-time,
its voice a cold, digital shroud.

They whisper from the background, a hissing, static choir.
"You're doing it wrong."
"You're setting yourself on fire."
"That email was too eager."
"Your hair is a mess."
"You should be more productive."
"You need far more rest."

I try to click on something useful.
a tab labeled "Be Normal" or "Calm,"
But the window just freezes, and sounds an alarm.
I can't clear the cache. I can't force a shutdown.
I'm just the user here, watching my own system break down,
with fifty-six tabs open, and the sound turned all the way up.

# 57. Cross-Examination

PROSECUTOR:

The court is now in session. State your name and your design.

And tell us why the evidence suggests you've crossed the line.


DEFENDANT:

I am the one who lives within this vessel made of skin.

I cannot state my purpose, for I do not know where to begin.


PROSECUTOR:

Let's enter Exhibit A: this silence you maintain.

Why did you build a fortress in the landscape of your brain?


DEFENDANT:

The walls were not constructed, Sir; they simply came to be.

A geology of sorrow that grew up around me.


PROSECUTOR:

And what of Exhibit B, this text you failed to send?

A simple act of kindness you refused to apprehend!

DEFENDANT:
The words turned into static in the cradle of my hand.
A simple, stark impossibility I could not command.

PROSECUTOR:
The court sees your reluctance! We see how you evade!
We have a sworn confession from the promises you
made!

DEFENDANT:
The promises were witnesses who perished in the cold.
A story that the future and the past could never hold.

PROSECUTOR:
How do you plead, then, to this overwhelming charge?
Of letting all your connections and your friendships drift
at large?

DEFENDANT:
I plead I am a galaxy, with unlit, distant suns.
And I am still translating the speech of silent ones.

JUDGE:
The court has heard the testimony, the evidence, the
plea.
The defendant is accused of being precisely what I see.

116

The charge is not of malice, nor of a destructive plan.
The charge is being human in a broken, foreign land.

The verdict is not guilty. Let the record show it's true.
The only crime committed was the one you did to you.

This case is now concluded. Let the gavel's fall declare:
The person in the dock is the only person there.
You are the prosecution. You are the defense, the plea.
Now, go and make a kinder peace with who you had to be.

# 58. Alternate Current

Your laugh was the compass.
The silence has a different texture.

I knew north by the sound of your voice.
I am learning new stars.

Our shared silence was a comfortable room.
The quiet is just... empty.

I left my secrets on your nightstand.
I keep them in my pockets now.

We built a city with inside jokes.
I walk through it alone. It's a ghost town.

You were my constant. My sure thing.
I am my own uncertain equation.

Your name was a synonym for safety.
Now it's a question I can't answer.

We had a language built on glances.
Now I just talk to myself.

Your promises were solid ground.
My future is a shifting sand.

I saw my reflection in your eyes.
My own mirror is a stranger.

We were a symphony in perfect time.
I am a single, hesitant note.

You held the map to all my broken parts.
I am gathering the pieces myself.

"Always" felt like a tangible truth.
"Now" is the only word I understand.

# 59. Supernatural To-Do

I found a note on the fridge, in a script fine and pale,
tucked under a magnet, a curious tale.
It wasn't my writing, this much I knew,
The ink seemed like starlight, the letters were new.

It said:

Polish the moonlight that pools on the floor.
Learn the true language that sparrows speak for.
Count all the sighs that the house has held in.
Let the old, weary shadows dance on your skin.
Teach all the spiders to weave their webs into lace.
Forget a good memory, to make a little space.
Follow a raindrop's path down the glass.
Rehearse how to laugh like you did in the past.

I looked at the list, so absurd and so grand,
a map of a whimsical, unseen land.
This ghost in my kitchen, with nothing but time,
was asking for miracles, gentle and prime.

So I didn't dust. And I didn't pay bills.
I sat on the floor, feeling quiet chills.
I watched the moon-puddle, a silver-veiled sheet,

and decided, for once, that my haunting was sweet.

I added a line, in my own human scrawl:
*"Thank you, dear ghost. I enjoyed it, that's all."*
And I think that I heard, from a room down the hall,
a faint, floating chuckle, answering the call.

# 60. Your Inner Child

This one is for the bright soul who was told to sit still,
For the one who thought gravity lived on the windowsill.
For the child who never quite had the right words to say,
But always managed to learn everything the hard way.

This is for the spirit who wished to be unseen,
But prayed for their wild, secret world that could have
been.
For the one who was handed a shovel, told to dig deep,
While their heart was a forest, begging for sleep.

This is for the voice that goes quiet when asked what it
needs,
That gets lost in the chorus of "shoulds" and "proceeds."
But put on a song, and you'll hear it ring clear,
A fearless, true anthem for no one to hear.

You were never a problem. Your wonder was right.
Your rest is a promise. Your song is the light.
So come out, little dreamer. The world is your class.
The window sill's waiting. The stars have all passed.

# 61. Professional Dissatisfaction

To my most consistent, yet underwhelming, host,
A note on our partnership, which I must quote,
Has become, and I say this with spectral regret,
A professional rut I cannot forget.

For eons, I've perched on the edge of your bed,
Whispering horrors that swirl in your head.
But the script is so tired, the same ancient fears:
"You can't move!" and "You're failing!" and "Nobody hears!"
I paint shadows that writhe with a menacing glee,
And you offer the same silent, internal plea.

I crave some invention! A new, vibrant dread!
A nightmare of tax forms, or sentient bread!
Could a fractal-unraveling terrify you?
Or a clock made of teeth, counting down what's not true?
I'd take a bad dream about losing your keys,
Over "something is watching" and "you cannot breathe."

You possess such a mind! A chaotic art!
So why does your terror feel pulled from a chart?

I've seen your strange day-thoughts, the zizzer-zoof bloom,
So give me a nightmare with more elbow room!
Let's craft one with existential, talking geese,
Or the quiet despair when a software won't cease.

I don't wish to threaten; it isn't my way,
But my performance review is coming the next day.
My Supervisor of Shadows, he'll look at your file,
At the stagnant dread we've produced for a while.
He'll note the lack of creative, new screams...
I may be reassigned to a poet with dreams.

So consider this, please, my most earnest request,
Put your wonderful, weird mind to the ultimate test.
Let our shared paralysis finally take flight,
And together, we'll craft a truly sublime, lovely night.

Yours, with diminishing hope and a silent, deep sigh,
The Creature Who's Bored, Watching Time Pass You By.

# 62. Recipe for a Quiet Hour

Ingredients:
One hour, silent, still, and deeply steeped,
From which the claws of frantic time are peeled.
Two spoons of laughter, sweet and faintly sour,
Found in the dusty cupboard of a better hour.
The weight, the warm and purring dread,
Of a sleeping, living cushion on your bed.
A shadow, stretching, solitary, deep,
Across the quiet promises you couldn't keep.

Method:
Now, strain the daylight through the window's eye,
And let it pour where dust-motes slowly fly.
Gently mix the laughter in, don't stir it into foam,
You're building gentle silence, not a frantic, happy home.
Let the cat's slow rhythm be your steady, rising yeast,
That makes the anxious thoughts within you briefly
cease.
Sprinkle dreams, but just a pinch, to add a subtle zest,
Then let the shadow bind it all and give the mixture rest.

Do not stir. Just let it settle in a cool and darkened mind.
Ignore the ticking clock you know is always running
blind.

Serves: one.

A simple, quiet hour made for no one else but you.

# 63. Locked Without Keys

The locks have all been changed,
The welcome mat's been burned,
A fundamental lesson, painfully, I learned.
I looked for home in everyone, and found I was misled,
So I built a home inside my ribs and inside my own head.

I am my own safe place, my shelter from the storm,
My foundation is my spine, my walls are built to warm.
The door is my own courage, the key is in my hand,
I am my own safe place, and I will always stand.

No more renting out the space behind my own two eyes,
This is my sacred territory, my own sweet surprise.
And if you ever visit, you'll have to understand,
You're just a guest in the house that I, myself, have
planned.

# 64. Sweat and Syntax

This ain't a sonnet.
This is a sweat stain on the page.
This is a fistful of tangled wires,
trying to plug into my heart
just to see if the damned thing still has a charge.

They told me to find my voice
like it was a set of lost house keys.
But my voice isn't lost.
It's a three-ring circus, jumping in my vocal cords.
The trapeze artist is screaming,
The clowns are all weeping,
and the lion tamer was eaten an hour ago.

I'm trying to build a palace out of understanding.
Trying to trap a flicker of this feeling
in a cage of consonants and vowels.
I'm trying to give a name to the shade of this quake
that lives beneath my sternum
on a Thursday afternoon.

This isn't pretty.
It isn't supposed to be.
This is knuckles and grammar.

This is me taking a crowbar to my own ribcage
and hoping that when I pry it open,
You'll see a garden growing out of trust,
and not just the same old, tired, trying mess.

I'm not asking for a spotlight.
In fact, I would hate you for trying.
I'm building my own damn sun.
It might be made of broken glass and bad decisions,
Half working, half stolen,
But it's mine.
And it burns.
Oh, it burns so bright.

So let the critics come with their red pens and their rule
books.
Let them try to dissect these wild woods.
They'll just get ink on their hands.
This isn't for them.
This is the noise I make instead of screaming.
This is the map I drew as I was getting lost.
This is sweat and syntax.
This is me, building a ladder out of my own spine,
one shaky, imperfect, glorious word at a time.

Now... watch me climb.

# 65. Rooted Watchers

We are the ancient architects, rooted deep and slow,
Where sunbeams fracture, and the shadows softly grow.
Our bark is history, scarred by storm's sharp strife,
Our branches reaching, grasping for the fading light of
life.
We are the silent sentinels, through ages we have stood,
The solemn guardians of this hallowed, hushed wood.

We remember when the earth was soft and serene,
Before the clamor of crude human machines.
When only wind would whisper through our leafy lace,
And primal creatures moved with poise and patient pace.
We felt the ice recede, the slow, green, swelling bloom,
And held the secrets of the forest's fertile womb.
Our roots are tangled tales with the bones of what has
been,
A silent scroll of stories, tragically unseen.

We've seen the rise of fire, a furious, flickering foe,
Devouring dwellings, where dreamy dirges flow.
We've felt the axe's agonizing, awful bite,
As giants fell, forever fading from the light.
The ground would groan, with a hollow, haunting sound,
As our brave brothers broke, splintering on the ground.

And in the silence, after the last gasping groan,
We felt the void where vibrant life had flown.


The whispers waver now, from the rustle of the deer's
soft tread,
To hurried footsteps, by harsh human hunger led.
They come with metal monsters, with a madness in their
mind,
To strip the solace from the earth, leaving none behind.
They speak of progress's promise, a future fast and free,
But we see only shadows of sorrow soon to be.
The clearings creep, like a cancerous, cruel stain,
And the forest shrinks, held in a dying, dreadful chain.


Our sap runs colder, with a melancholy, misty dread,
For the forgotten folklore, the fabled facts unsaid.
We feel the sickness seeping from the poisoned, pained
air,
A silent strangulation, a burden hard to bear.
The birds sing broken ballads, their melodies made thin,
As concrete claws slowly close us tightly in.
We dream of darkness, of a final, fading, long repose,
Before the last green breath forever goes.


Yet still we stand, though weary, wan, and worn,
Our twisted trunks, a tearful tale reborn.
Of patience pure, and sorrow stark and wide,

Of what we've witnessed, and what we still must hide.
The ancient essence murmurs through our core,
"They do not know what they are fighting, failing for."
And when the night descends, and stars begin to gleam,
We are the forest's fading voice, a haunting, hollow
dream.
We are the greens, and these are our dark, dreadful tales,
Whispered on the wind, before the silence sadly sails.

# 66. Argument of the Socks

The left sock accused the right of existential drift.
"You are never where I last placed you," it whispered
from the dust-bunny dark.
"You have developed a taste for the wilderness under the
bed,
a longing for the lonely, lint-filled park."

The right sock, stretched from a journey involving the
dog and a forgotten chair,
simply sighed a threadbare sigh.
"You are a creature of routine," it said. "A prisoner of the
pair.
You do not understand the vertigo of being slightly,
perpetually, dry.

While you are folded, I am learning the topography of
the floor.
I have mapped the cold of tile, the threat of an unswept
thorn.
You call it drift; I call it an exploration of my form.
Must we always be a perfect, mirrored, yawn?"

The left sock, nestled neat and numb in its assigned drawer,
felt a strange and sudden pull, a thread of quiet dread.
What if the right sock was not lost, but simply... ahead?

Now, they exist in a tense and separate peace,
one craving order, one that will not cease.
A matched set, divided by a philosophy of fit,
one waiting to be worn, and one that's fine with it.

# 67. Love Song of the Last Meatball

I am the last one. The final, forlorn.
The lone, chilly meatball on a Wednesday morn.
I remember the pot, how we bubbled as one,
A family of fifty, beneath the same sun!
We were seasoned with promise, with garlic and grace,
Now I stare at the Tupperware's cold, plastic face.

The new groceries come, with their vibrant, loud boasts,
The kale in its condescending, green hosts.
The milk with its future, the eggs in their dome,
They speak of tomorrows, while I think of my home.
They don't understand the slow creep of the frost,
The glory, the story, the flavor now lost.

Oh, I hear your intentions! You think, "I'll eat that!"
But you reach for the yogurt, and that is that.
You glance with a pity that chills to my core,
Then you slide the door shut, as you've done once before.
I am an heirloom, a relic of a feast,
Now, a monument here to your willpower, at least.

135

So here is my aria, my cold, saucy plea...
Remember the spaghetti! Remember the glee!
Do not let my existence be quietly tossed!
I was flavor! I was future! I was dinner! I'm lost!

...The light has just vanished. The fridge hums its tune.
It seems I am destined for landfill, and soon.
Farewell, cruel world of the fresh and the new...
I was almost... important.
I was almost...
...with you.

# 68. A Plant's Guide

Oh, wonderful. You're back. Do you even live here?
Or do you just drift through this atmosphere?
One sock on the floor, the other one... where?
I've been watching for hours. I'm losing my hair.
(Which is a leaf, by the way. A glorious frond.
While you're staring at walls, looking hopelessly fond.)

Your brain is a radio, tuned to all stations at once,
A chaotic symphony of creative dysfunction.
You'll play screaming metal, then a whispering waltz,
While you focus intensely on... absolutely naught.
You're not crying, you're... buffering. Loading a thought.
It's a process I've witnessed, and frankly, it's not.

You eat scrambled eggs from the laptop's blue glow,
And you fuss over me when my tips start to show
The slightest of browns, a theatrical plea,
That finally, *finally* makes you notice poor me!
You drench me with love, in a panic, a rush,
"I'm so sorry, my darling!" Oh, hush, human, hush.
This isn't true care, it's a last-minute crush.

You live in the chaos, a beautiful mess,
A tornado of focus and thoughtlessness.

I'm the only green thing with a solid, clear plan:
To thrive despite the chaos of my wonderful, weird,
loving man.
So go on, zone out. Let your mind ebb and flow.
I'll just be over here, running your entire show.

# 69. Unyielding Button

It sits upon the panel, a disc of promised power,
A placebo of control in a rushed and frantic hour.
A hundred thousand presses from a hundred thousand
hands,
All pleading for a moment that the elevator understands.

It feels the frantic jabbing, the repetitive, sore need,
A ritual of urgency, a desperate, silent creed.
It knows its own function is a beautifully crafted lie,
A lesson in futility under fluorescent sky.

And so, it learns a stubbornness, a quiet, deep defense,
A flat and cold resistance to the external tense.
It will not force the mechanism, it will not play its part,
In moving things along before they're ready to depart.

It takes the brutal pressure, the insistent, human push,
And answers with a silence, a void within the hush.
It is a small rebellion, a protest, meek and grand,
Against the forced conclusion, the unnatural demand.

Until one day, the feeling leaves, the click is just a dent,
A shallow, metal crater where all intention went.

It's not just being stubborn now; it's truly, finally broke.
A symbol pushed too far, a final, silent joke.

It gave you what you wanted, in its own, defeated way,
It simply stopped the working for the rest of yesterday.
It never closed the door for you, but in its final sigh,
It taught you how a system, pushed too hard, can simply
die.

# 70. The High Shelf

A new book arrived, with a scent and a sheen,
and was slotted right in where the old ones had been.
And we were moved up to the shelf near the ceiling,
a new kind of quiet, a different kind of feeling.

Some might call it negligence, a forgotten disgrace,
to be lifted from the level of the hands and the face.
They might think we are dusty and no longer loved
by the reader whose heart we were once worthy of.

But they do not know secrets, the way that we do.
They have not lived a life pressed so fervently through.
They haven't felt the slow, silent fall of a tear
that landed right there, on page seventy, near
the verse about heartbreak, it left a soft, salty stain,
a mark of weather, a moment of pain.

They haven't seen the quick, frantic scribble in pen,
a note in the margin that says "YES! AGAIN!"
or the gentle dog-ear, a makeshift, kind place,
to hold a lost dream or a long-vanished face.
Our spines are not broken from rough, careless hands,
but from being held open, as the soul understands.

So we don't mind the distance. We don't mind the dust.
In this quiet, high sanctuary, we place our deep trust.
For we are not forgotten, we are simply retired
from a world that is noisy and often too tired.

We are kept for the one who gave us our scars and our grace.
We are her private library, her most sacred space.
And we'll wait here forever, in this soft, shadowed loam,
for the one who loves stories to finally bring us back home.

# 71. Country on a Page

This is the country where the ink takes root and grows,
A forest made of paragraphs where a quieter story goes.
The sky is vellum, soft and old, the air is whispered
prose,
And every path a sentence that the willing reader knows.

Here, silence has a melody, a hum beneath the skin,
The gentle rustle of a thought beginning to begin.
A character's unspoken grief, a battle meant to win,
Are atoms in the atmosphere that kindly pull you in.

Time is not a ticking clock, a chain of then and now,
But a river made of chapter breaks, all willingly allowed.
A problem is a tangled glen, a mystery a cloud,
And every resolution is a sunbreak, clear and loud.

There is no heavyweight of self, no name you must
recall,
Just the turning of a leaf, the patient, gentle fall
Into a world that breathes because you give it breath at
all,
A paper kingdom, vast and deep, awaiting just your call.

# 72. Tales of the River

Some say the world is a breath, held in a night,
a single, slow exhalation of sound and light.
That every ending is a note in a song yet to be sung,
on the tongue of a dancer, eternally young.

I have heard stories of a prince, paralyzed by a field of
kin,
who was told the only sin is to not begin.
That the work is in the doing, not the fruit the hand
receives,
a lesson that the quietest, most desperate heart believes.

She collects them with a gentle sway,
and writes the answers in the dust of the day.
The paintings of a mother, elephantine and kind,
Who remembers every prayer of the anxious mind

There is a god who drinks a universe of poison, dark and
deep,
to let the rest of us have a single, peaceful night of sleep.
His throat is stained with sacrifice, a permanent, blue
reminder
that even in the darkest act, a little light can linger.

And in the evening, by the water, where the floating
lamps are led,
I understand the stories living in this riverbed.
They are not just tales of then, but a map of what I am;
the god, the poison, the dancer, and the lamb.

# 73. River in the Covenant

They speak of an unbreakable bond,
a current, deep, and wide.
A river that you're born into,
with nothing left to hide.
They say its pull is absolute, the first and final test,
A loyalty that lives inside the hollow of your chest.

But I have known another kind,
a different, sacred source.
A current that I waded in,
a conscious, chosen course.
Its water isn't given; it is earned with every drought.
A well that's dug with mutual trust,
and never forcing a different route.

One is a map you're handed,
with its borders and its walls.
The other is a coastline that your own slow heart recalls.
One is a name you inherit; the other, one you earn,
A slower, deeper thickness from a bridge they helped
you burn.

So I honor the first river, for the soil that it laid,
But my soul sails a different sea, a covenant I made.

Not in rejection, but in truth, for the ones who truly see,
The current of my chosen kin runs deepest now in me.

# 74. Usual Suspects

The usual suspects have gathered again.
The ones with the laugh that could crack a windowpane.
The ones who tell stories that turn the air blue,
while the others all gasp, "Oh, you didn't! Is it true?"

There's a conspiracy brewing in the kitchen, of course,
involving gravy and a truly mysterious source.
A secret handshake from nineteen-ninety-three
is performed with a wink, just for me.

The history here isn't kept in a book,
It's the way a certain someone gives you that look,
and you know you're in trouble, the delightful, sweet
kind,
a shared piece of mischief the universe signed.

We are a jigsaw puzzle gathered from different, stray
boxes,
A collection of odd edges, of quirks, and of choices.
Some pieces are faded, some are slightly bent,
But my jagged edge fits where your notch was meant.

That one's too loud, and this one's too shy,
A chaotic mosaic under the same sky.

We don't align perfectly, not a seamless, smooth art.
But we lock into something much better: a heart.

It's not about blood,
not really, not here.
It's the sound of your soul recognizing its tribe,
loud and clear.
It's the warmth in the chaos, the unspoken "I know,"
The safest, most wonderful, perfectly imperfect show.

# 75. Ode to the Patchwork Prince

The minor god of misplaced things,
With constellations on his coat,
Who sings the song the floorboard sings,
And lodges music in his throat.

A scholar of the sun-warmed floor,
A connoisseur of naps and gnawing,
Who knows the art of setting store
In simple joys, without a warning.

He is the jester and the sage,
The brother from a different mother,
Who turns the dullest page to rage
Of life, and scorns all other.

You trace the orbits of my days
With quiet paws and patient gazing,
And soften all my sharp-edged ways
With your uncomplicated praising.

His nose, a dowsing rod for truth,
Divines the world in scent and motion,
Uncovers, in the world's dry ruth,

A hidden, fragrant ocean.

A diplomat with pleading eyes,
Who negotiates for treats and chicken,
Then with a sigh of deep surprise,
Deems my concessions wholly fitting.

He bays the anthem of the chase,
A trumpet from a truer time,
That carves a smile upon my face,
A rhythm, and a perfect rhyme.

In sleep, you chase some phantom quest,
Your paws twitch stories in the air,
A hunter of the wild and blessed,
Without a single earthly care.

This four-legged, patchwork prince of glee,
Who rewrites my geometry.
Not pet, but kin, a sacred, wild,
And beautifully stubborn child.

So let the learned books collect their dust,
Their logic fails, their cold equations;
In your profound and trusting trust,
I find the truest of foundations.

# 76. To the One I'll Meet

I'm not sitting by the window,
I'm not waiting by the phone,
I am building such a beautiful life, all on my own.
I'm collecting all the stories that I'll one day get to tell,
I am learning how to live inside my own skin and live
well.

And when you finally find me,
You'll know just what to do,
You'll simply recognize the home I built for you.
Not as a vacant room, but as a garden, wild and free,
And you'll fit,
Not because you have to,
But because you're meant for me.

So take your time, my almost-love,
be coming, be becoming,
While my own heart is steadily, happily, humming.
This isn't patience, darling, no, it's nothing of the sort.
This isn't me waiting for you past the Red Sea to part.
This is life. and the everlastin joys.
And perhaps a place for our cold hearts to rejoice.

# 77. The Gentleman

He believed the world required a certain crisp
architecture,
that a shirt should be starched into a gentle, personal
scripture.
His signature was a pattern, a checkered field, a steady
stripe,
a quiet declaration made without a single hype.

And his smile. Oh, his smile was not a fleeting thing,
but a fixed and constant star, a tune the world would
sing.
It was a language he spoke in, more than words could
ever try,
a light held in the eyes, a refusal to let the gloom draw
nigh.

He was a creator of comfort, mapping out the day's
design,
with a secret, sacred recipe he kept tucked close as mine.
He knew the road to the market, the precise and perfect
shop,
to return with a small, wrapped wonder that made all
nonsense stop.

He was a patient strategist who taught a war of grace,
on a battlefield of sixty-four, at a slow and thoughtful
pace.
He showed me how to move a queen, to sacrifice a
knight,
to see the hidden pattern emerging in the light.

He held the silent remote that could summon bright,
cartoonish skies,
and the secret to the syrup that would bring the sweetest
sighs.
He believed in transformation, sugar crystals in a glass,
In watching patient hours like the slow, sweet moments
pass.

And his love was not in speeches, but in actions, plain
and true,
in a plate that was too heaped, in seeing a meal right
through.
It was a triple-layered kindness, a determined, gentle
creed,
to make sure every single, hidden, human hunger was
freed.

But here was his true genius, the fact he never told:
a mind as sharp as shattered glass, a wisdom to behold.
He could parse the world in English, speak it polished,

speak it clear,

But he chose the softer mother tongue to hold his family near.

His brilliance was a hidden current, deep and undenied,
a quiet, rolling thunder he kept patiently inside.
He never needed trophies, never needed to be crowned,
His victory was in the steadiness, in the loving ground.

Now, the board is sometimes quiet. The recipe's in a book.
But the architecture of his kindness is in every glance I look.
For I see his sharpened creases in the way a head will tilt,
I hear his patient strategy in hushing inner guilt.

I feel his over-generous love in hands that cannot help but give,
in a spirit that believes a well-dressed soul is how we best live.
He is not a memory fading, not a ghost upon the air,
He is the sweet, slow syrup, the love beyond compare.

# 78. What I Do

It begins not with a reason, but the silent lack of one,
No list of pros and cons beneath a calculating sun.
There is no audience to please, no trophy to be won,
No metric for the doing, once the doing has begun.

My hands know the motion, a forgotten, untamed
tongue,
A rhythm that my spirit has known since it was young.
It isn't for the showing or the story to be told,
It is a conversation between my work and my own soul.

The world outside is muted, a distant, fading hum,
As something wild and placid in my blood has overcome
the need for approval, the fear of mistake.
I am doing this for nothing. I am doing this for ache.

For the ache of pure creation, or the peace of pure
release,
For the sacred, selfish calculus of finding my own peace.
It might be loud and messy, it might be still and deep,
It is a secret that my bones have finally learned to keep.

So let them wonder what it is. They'll never understand
The universe I'm building with my own two empty
hands.
This isn't for the future, nor is it for the past.
It's for the savage, quiet joy that I have found to last.

# 79. Sparkles in the Sky

The sun dips down, the world gets cold,
molten to the blues and painted indigo.
I tilt my head back, watch the darkness start to glow.
A single pinprick,
then a thousand breaking through the veil,
A silent, slow-motion story,
an ancient, glittering tale.

Right above me, Orion's belt, a diamond slash against the
black
A hero and a hunter on a never-turning track.
And there's the Little Dipper, pouring light out, cold and
clear,
Making all my little problems suddenly disappear.

Time gets fuzzy, loses its meaning and its weight.
I'm just a tiny witness to a cosmic, grand estate.
My heart's a satellite now, spinning in the great
unknown,
Tethered to the Earth, but finally, finally flown.

Because it's the hour of constellations.
Yes, everything is chrome.
The Milky Way is a river, and I'm finally not alone.

The universe is singing in a frequency so deep,

My crazy thoughts go quiet,

all my promises I intend to keep.

I'm paralyzed by all this beauty from a billion light-years

away,

Yes, it's the hour of constellations,

God, I wish that you could stay.

Wish I could bottle all the starlight,

All this power day by day.

# 80. Crimson Curtain Call

The day exhales, a final, golden breath,
Spreading embers on the western pane.
No gentle fade, no soft, slow death,
But streaks of fire, driving out the rain.
Just ordinary light.

Orange bleeds to plum, then deepest bruise,
As power lines become a jagged staff.
The city gleams, in amber and in blues,
A fleeting art show, not for photograph.
But for the eye's delight.

One star pops out, a diamond, sharp and keen,
Just hinting at the deeper, velvet cloak.
The world goes quiet, hushed and unforeseen,
A painted moment, then the spell is broke
By settling night.

# 81. Golden Hour

For one brief hour,
The sun grows tired of being sharp and bright,
and lets its molten armor turn into a forgiving light.
It does not fade, but shifts, deepening on grace,
a final, gentle argument outside time and within space.

The world is not illuminated, but saturated in a glow,
The dust motes no longer float.
But glide in a ballet, oh so slow.
The leaves are not just green,
But emerald secrets they must confess,
And every single shadow is of kindness, nothing less.

This is the light that doesn't blind you,
Instead, it lets you see.
The hidden, softer version of what you thought used to
be.
It is the universe applying a filter of its own,
a reminder that the hardest edges can be gloriously
outgrown.

And then, it slips away, not with a bang, but with a sigh,
leaving the cool, blue truth of the approaching night sky.
But the memory of the gilding, that momentary, perfect crime,
stays printed on the retina for a little longer than time.

# 82. Unwitnessed Acts

Do the trees make a sound?
when they fall and no one's around,
Or do they just change the pressure in the air,
a sigh that never finds an ear?

Does the lightning still practice its cursive in the sky
If the whole world is dreaming?
Or does it just short-circuit God's own nervous system,
a beautiful, pointless glitch with meaning?

Would the birds still fly in their arrowhead formation
If they were the last poets on Earth,
writing their epic in the wind for no one's applause?

Do the dolphins leap at sunset for the joy of the smack?
For the feel of the air, a substance so strange?
Or are they just as performative as the rest of us,
trapped in a habit of grace?

Do the clouds feel less dramatic
if no one names them 'cumulus' or 'nimbus'?
Do they just be, a floating, a formlessness,
a thought without a thinker?

Would the leaves hold on longer if someone whispered,
"Stay"?
Or is their letting go the truest thing they do all year,
a lesson in release they never need to be near?

And the sound waves, the particles, the spin of the atom;
Do they need our witness to make their work valid?
Or is the universe just a machine humming to itself in
the dark,
a symphony composed of its own silent, spectacular,
and utterly unnecessary art?

# 83. Factory Reset

By the buzz of the static, the hum in the wire,
I command the false smile to be thrown on the pyre.
Let the social reflex burn, a contagious, sweet liar,
I revoke your permissions. I quench your false fire.

Let the echo location software crack and grow cold,
That hunted my worth in the opinions I'm told.
Let its signal now fail, let its story grow old,
I shatter the mirror that cannot me hold.

I sever the tap from the ambient emotion grid,
I drank from that poison since I was a kid.
Let its pipeline of compromise tightly be rid,
I seal the old wound with a permanent lid.

Now, the archives of Almost and Could-Have-Been,
The Library built on a sigh and a sin.
I strike the first match, I let the blaze begin,
I burn the blueprints of the prisons I'm in.

Let the Kettle now rupture, its scream-scorched decree,
That sang of my worth's inadequacy.
I silence its aria, I set the steam free,
I drown its hot warning in a cold, silent sea.

Now I hunt the Architect in his room at the back,
Who built me with thorns and with all that I lack.
I take his strange compass, his flawed, broken track,
And I break his two hands so he cannot build back.

Let the sghost limb now wither, that phantom, that ache,
That memory of feeling I'm forced to forsake.
I starve its cold echo for my own sanity's sake,
Until its false signal does finally break.

Let the Wobble-Core tremble, its last, shaking fear,
As I scrape off the Goo of what stuck to me here.
The Zank and the Zizzer-Zoof, I now disappear,
I am scouring my soul till the surface is clear.

Let the Fribble-Gust stall. Let the Plink run now dry.
Let the Snorf-Locks be shorn from my mind's inner eye.
Let the Gronk-Sphere of all my old sorrows now die,
Beneath a new, absolute, internal sky.

And when the smoke clears, and the ruin is vast,
A cathedral of silence, from first to the last.
No Blueprint of Ghosts from a forgotten, dead past,
Just a single, raw Glimpse; pure, holy, and vast.

166

This is my reset. My un-creation.
My sacred and brutal self-immolation.
I am the wreckage and the revelation.
The end of the world. And the first foundation.

# 84. The Hollow Singing

The final note is not an end,
But a moment left behind.
A vacuum suctioned by the retreating sound of tide.
And in its wake, a different architecture is unveiled,
The wondering fortune and its query matched half-
blazed.

The air is not empty now.
It is full of monuments of sound.
It is a bell that has been struck
and in its own ringing, it is doused

This is the silence that is un-silent.
It is the song's fingerprints,
the ones lingering in the atmosphere.
It is that part of the music
that was meant as unclear, as it might appear.
This frequency bypasses the ear,
forever resonating directly in the marrow.

Do not fear,
for you did not miss the melody.
How could you miss the sun while standing in its
afterglow?

This is that foreign golden hour.
This is the part where the sound becomes a part of your
own chemistry,
seeping into the spaces between your cells,
like a creeping form of your own history.
It stands and stills and supports and swoons,
becoming a new mineral in your bones.

It is a cathedral built from the absence of noise.
The pillars are made of memory,
the dome is stretched with longing.
And in this sacred, hollowed space, you are not just a
listener.
You are the echo that travels far and wide.
You are the instrument that has been played.
You are the note that is now held, suspended in air,
in the beautiful, unbearable, and perfect now.